Epitaphs Of A Dying Sun

Yasir Alam

India | USA | UK

Made with ❤ on the BookLeaf Publishing Platform
www.bookleafpub.in
www.bookleafpub.com

Dedication

*To the restless souls,
the ones who question,
the ones who seek meaning in
the noise.
To those who find beauty in the
chaos,
and to those who dare to
confront the silence—
this one's for you.
May the flicker of your own light
never fade.*

Preface

Epitaphs of a Dying Sun is not a collection of poems, but a journey. A journey through the echoes of our own existence, through the shifting shadows and fleeting flickers that make up the fabric of our lives. This book is a reflection, an exploration of the contrasts between life's vibrancy and its inevitable stillness, between our fleeting joys and the crushing weight of time.

Each chapter, each poem, is a glimpse into a different corner of this experience, pulling at the threads of what it means to exist, to love, to suffer, and to eventually fade away. The names you'll read are more than just titles. They are markers of the stages of life we all traverse, whether knowingly or not.

It's not about the answers, it's about the questions. Not about the destination, but the journey.

In a world where the light burns bright, the flicker of the dying sun serves as a reminder that all things must pass. And so we walk, we burn, and we fade.

Acknowledgements

To the void that inspired every line, every thought—thank you for your endless presence, your silence, your wisdom.

To the restless dreamers who never let go of their questions, who never stopped searching for meaning in the chaos—this is your reflection too.

To my family, who taught me that even the darkest night can hold fragments of light. Your love and support keep me grounded, even when the world feels like it's slipping away.

To my closest friends, those who've listened to me vent and pour out my soul in moments of doubt and fear—you've carried me, even when I couldn't carry myself.

And **to every reader** who picks up these pages and dives into the deep end of uncertainty—**thank you** for walking this road with me. You are the reason this book exists. May it echo in your mind, even when the words are gone.

1. The Last Rays

The sun's last kiss upon the earth,
A fleeting warmth, a burst of mirth,
As day departs, the shadows grow,
A final dance in golden glow.
The sky, once bright, begins to fade,
The hues of pink begin to trade,
For purple shades, for darkened blue,
The twilight bids the world adieu.
Beneath the warmth, the world stands still,
Whispers of hope, a dying thrill,
A promise that it's not the end,
Yet we know, it's only pretend.
For even stars, they bow and fall,
And love, too, faces this cold call—
We chase the light that fades so slow,
Unaware, the darkness grows.
A world that shone, now lost in time,
Its beauty fades in silent rhyme,
The last rays kiss the earth's worn cheek,
And in their wake, all hopes are weak.
Yet still we cling, with trembling hands,
To the light, like forgotten sands,
For when the night falls, cold and deep,
What once we held, we cannot keep.

The last rays fall, and so do we,
Like leaves adrift on a bitter sea.

2. Flickering Light

There was a time, a time of gold,
When warmth would rise, unbought, untold,
The flickers of the coming night,
Were still just whispers in the light.
Yet now those flickers are so near,
A warning signal, loud and clear.
The sun, once bold, begins to bend,
The dawn is close—its light shall end.
In every corner, every crack,
The dark encroaches, no turning back.
A flicker here, a flicker there,
A sign of hope, then none to spare.
But still we wait, as if to say,
That flicker's here to light the way.
Yet even flickers die with time,
Their embers burning out in rhyme.
The flickers are the dreams we keep,
Promises too fragile, too deep.
We see them, chase them, hold them tight,
But none can hold the fading light.
A dance of shadows, faint and brief,
A trembling sigh, a whispered grief.
The flicker dies; it fades away,
The night arrives to steal the day.

And we, the watchers, stand in vain,
Grasping at light, but feeling pain.

3. Shadows Beneath the Glow

Shadows grow where light once shone,
Darkness crawling, flesh and bone,
It whispers, calls, a silent plea,
A tug, a pull, toward misery.
Beneath the glow of dying light,
We see the truth in endless night—
The things we thought were pure and bright,
Now tarnished, gone, out of sight.
Once bathed in gold, we now descend,
The light that warmed us meets its end.
The shadows speak of what's to come,
A bitter truth, a drumming hum.
Beneath the glow, we know the cost,
The path ahead is already lost.
The colors once so vivid, bold,
Now washed away, turned pale and cold.
The shadows stretch, they twist, they creep,
In every corner, dark thoughts sleep.
A dance of death in every turn,
A quiet, steady, slow burn.
We walk between the light and dark,
Chasing hope, but leaving a mark.
For every step toward the light,

We take two more into the night.
The glow may flicker, faint, undone,
But shadows rise where once was sun.

4. Fading Footprints

The ground we walk, it holds our names,
Our steps are carved, our fleeting games.
But with each step, the prints grow thin,
The memories we keep, they sin.
For though we leave our mark, our trace,
It vanishes without a face.
The footsteps fade, the sands erase,
The earth no longer holds its place.
Once there was laughter in the halls,
But now the silence heavily falls.
We look behind, but none remain,
The footsteps lost in falling rain.
A life once full of vibrant sound,
Now hollow echoes all around.
The prints we left will turn to dust,
And in that dust, our hopes will rust.
We leave behind what once we knew,
A path once bright, now veiled in blue.
Our feet still move, but where to go?
A journey lost in winds that blow.
And so we fade, like footprints light,
Into the shadows, out of sight.

5. Between the Dusk and Dawn

The world hangs still, suspended here,
Between the dusk and dawn's own fear.
Neither night nor day, just wait,
A pause before the heavy weight.
The sky a canvas torn in two,
A battle between red and blue.
The sun will rise, the moon will fall,
And in between, we feel it all.
The world is neither dark nor bright,
But stuck in that forgotten light.
The space between, where thoughts collide,
Where truth and lies cannot divide.
The waiting seems so endless, vast,
For time, once still, is now so fast.
We wait for dawn, but dread its call,
For what if dawn brings naught at all?
The world in limbo, stuck, confused,
By truths once known, now so abused.
The dusk and dawn are worlds apart,
But live together, heart to heart.
And in this space, we long for more—
A place between, forever poor.

6. The Hollow Echo

The winds that whispered long ago,
Now echo hollow, soft and slow.
The songs they sang, the words they told,
Now lost in echoes, faint and cold.
The world once full of life and sound,
Now mute, where silence does abound.
The voice that once could lift us high,
Now fades beneath the empty sky.
In every corner, in every mind,
The echoes call, they twist and wind.
A memory, a face, a name,
A fleeting glimpse, forever tame.
But the echoes never cease,
They call us back to our disease.
The hollow call, the distant sound,
The emptiness that knows no bound.
We search for answers, yet we find,
The echoes left us far behind.
A voice, a call, a fleeting dream,
Now lost within the silent scream.
The echoes stretch, they pull us near,
A world undone, a life unclear.

7. The Dying Breath

Breathe in deep, the air so thin,
A fragile life, so frail within.
The world is still, the earth so cold,
Its heartbeat weak, its pulse grows old.
Each breath we take, each fleeting sigh,
A step closer to the sky.
The wind no longer feels the same,
A quiet loss, a whispered name.
The breath we take, the breath we leave,
A fleeting chance to mourn or grieve.
For in each moment, death is near,
A shadow lurking, always here.
The world that once was loud and bright,
Now dims beneath the dying light.
Each breath we take, each moment lost,
A price we pay, no matter cost.
Yet still we breathe, though faint, though weak,
A dying hope, a broken streak.
And in the end, when breath is gone,
What's left behind? A life undone.
The dying breath, the final toll,
A hollow whisper fills the soul.

8. The Cold Embrace

A touch so cold, it chills the skin,
A hand that reaches deep within.
The warmth once known, now lost to night,
A frozen grasp, devoid of light.
The cold embrace that pulls us near,
A touch of death, a touch of fear.
No warmth to hold, no hand to keep,
Just endless night, just endless sleep.
It pulls us close, it drags us down,
A crown of ice, a frozen crown.
In every heart, it plants its seed,
A longing that we cannot feed.
The cold embrace will never let,
The warmth we sought, the hope we met.
It drags us under, deep below,
Where nothing lives, where nothing grows.
And in the dark, we're left to freeze,
A frozen soul, a dying breeze.
The cold embrace, forever near,
A constant reminder of our fear.
The warmth is gone, the touch so cold,
A heart that's lost, a life grown old.

9. The Silent Storm

A storm within, but none to see,
A battle fought so silently.
The rage, the fire, it burns inside,
But no one knows, it cannot hide.
The sky above, it swells with might,
But here below, there's not a sight.
The winds that howl, the thunder's roar,
Are lost within, forevermore.
The silent storm that rages on,
A broken heart, a battle drawn.
No eyes to witness, no ears to hear,
The pain that lingers, sharp and clear.
It churns inside, it twists, it tears,
A storm of thoughts, of silent prayers.
The winds may blow, the earth may quake,
But this storm's depth, none can take.
The silent storm will never cease,
It eats away, it gives no peace.
And though we fight, and though we scream,
It rages on, an endless dream.
The storm inside, a silent fear,
No way to stop, no way to steer.

10. The Withering Garden

Once a bloom, so bright and fair,
Now withered, gone, beyond repair.
The petals fall, the roots decay,
The garden fades, it slips away.
The flowers that once kissed the sun,
Now bow their heads, their day is done.
The colors lost, the fragrance gone,
A garden wilts, it lingers on.
Once full of life, a vibrant hue,
Now pale and tired, through and through.
The garden withers, the trees bow low,
The life once strong, now moves so slow.
The leaves fall softly to the ground,
A silent sorrow all around.
The wind no longer whispers sweet,
It brings only sorrow, cold defeat.
In every corner, life retreats,
The garden fades in quiet beats.
And as it dies, so do we,
For this garden mirrors you and me.
The bloom is gone, the petals fall,
The garden whispers, "This is all."

11. The Shattered Mirror

A reflection cracked, a shattered view,
The pieces scattered, broken through.
The face I knew, no longer clear,
A mask of doubt, a trace of fear.
The glass once whole, a perfect frame,
Now fractured, lost, without a name.
Each shard a story, each piece a lie,
A fractured soul, a hollow sky.
The mirror whispers, soft, so cold,
A thousand truths that we've been told.
Yet none are real, none hold the key,
To unlock the door, to set us free.
I reach for the pieces, but they slip,
A fleeting hope, a tightening grip.
The mirror mocks, the glass distorts,
Reflecting all our twisted thoughts.
In every crack, a shattered dream,
A life undone, a broken scream.
But we still search, we still believe,
That through the cracks, we can retrieve.
The shattered mirror, the broken view,
Reflects the self, the hidden you.

12. The Hollow Heart

A heart once full, now cold and bare,
The warmth is gone, the love's not there.
The beating slows, the pulse grows weak,
A hollow void, a life so bleak.
The walls I built, they crack and fall,
The echo fades, no answer calls.
The love once known, a distant sound,
Now lost beneath the empty ground.
The hollow heart, the aching beat,
A rhythm slow, incomplete.
It once was filled with joy and light,
Now lost to shadows, lost to night.
And though I search, and though I try,
I cannot fill the space inside.
The hollow heart will never mend,
It beats alone, until the end.
A heart so still, a soul so dry,
The hollow waits, the hollow cries.

13. The Fading Echoes

The whispers fade, the voices lost,
A memory, a fleeting cost.
The words once heard, now faint, now gone,
A broken echo, a fading song.
The silence spreads, it fills the air,
A stillness deep, a heavy care.
The sound that once could lift the soul,
Now lost within the deepened hole.
The echoes fade, they fade so slow,
But leave behind the undertow.
A tug, a pull, a hidden plea,
A cry for help we cannot see.
But in the quiet, there's a sound,
A distant rumble, soft, profound.
The fading echoes still remain,
A haunting hum, a soft refrain.
The echoes slip, the voices die,
Yet still they linger, still they lie.

14. The Broken Clock

The ticking stops, the hands stand still,
A frozen time, a broken will.
The hours pass, yet none shall move,
A clock that ceases, a heart that proves.
The moments once so full, so bright,
Now stretch to endless, empty night.
The seconds slip, the minutes crawl,
The broken clock, it tells it all.
The future lost, the past erased,
A moment gone, a dream displaced.
The time that passed is lost to me,
The clock that stands, eternally.
And though we wait, and though we long,
The time once lost cannot belong.
The broken clock, a frozen stare,
A life suspended, caught in air.
The ticking's gone, the silence grows,
The broken time, the time that knows.

15. The Silent Requiem

No song to sing, no tear to shed,
A requiem for the soul long dead.
The silence speaks, the stillness calls,
A hollow echo, as life falls.
The music once so sweet and pure,
Now lost to time, a fading cure.
No notes remain, no sounds arise,
Just empty space, beneath dark skies.
The requiem plays, but none can hear,
A silent song, a whispered fear.
The melody of life undone,
A tune that's lost, a race not won.
The silent requiem plays so slow,
A funeral march, a final blow.
And though we long to hear its grace,
The silence steals, it leaves no trace.
The song is gone, the notes erased,
A requiem without a face.

16. The Lonely Lantern

A flicker, faint, a dying glow,
The lantern's light, so soft, so low.
It once burned bright, it once shone true,
Now lost beneath the shades of blue.
The wind that blew, the rain that poured,
The lantern's flame, the light it ignored.
It flickers weak, it flickers faint,
A dimmed resolve, a tired saint.
The lantern struggles, still it fights,
To hold its flame against the night.
But in the dark, it fades away,
A light that cannot see the day.
The lonely lantern, standing tall,
Fighting shadows, fighting all.
But in the end, it flickers out,
A lone star lost in endless doubt.
The light is gone, the dark remains,
A lantern lost, a heart in chains.

17. The Weeping Sky

The sky above, it weeps for me,
A silent cry, a misery.
The clouds, they bleed, the stars they fall,
A tear-streaked sky, a shattered call.
The rains pour down, the heavens weep,
A sorrow deep, a pain so steep.
No sun, no light, just endless grey,
The sky mourns what it cannot say.
The weeping sky, the tears it sheds,
For dreams once held, for hopes once fed.
And though we wait for skies to clear,
The clouds remain, the pain sincere.
The sky, it cries, it knows our name,
A sorrow deep, a burning flame.
But in the weeping, we're not free,
For even heavens long to flee.
The tears fall down, the sky is torn,
A mourning world, a soul reborn.

18. The Quietus

A stillness comes, so soft, so slow,
The quietus calls, the end we know.
No cries, no screams, no desperate plea,
Just calm, just peace, just endless sea.
The world falls silent, all is still,
A quiet end, a hollow fill.
No fear, no dread, no trembling hands,
Just quietude that understands.
The quietus whispers, soft and kind,
A release from all that's left behind.
No pain, no loss, no hurt to bear,
Just peace, a moment free of care.
And as we sink into the night,
The quietus wraps us in its light.
No fear, no sorrow, just release,
The quietus brings eternal peace.
The quiet falls, the silence reigns,
A calm that heals, a soul that wanes.

19. The Final Flicker

The light grows dim, the end is near,
A final flicker, a fading cheer.
The embers burn, they slowly die,
A spark that once lit up the sky.
The world is quiet, the air is still,
The flicker flicks, against its will.
It once was bright, it once was bold,
Now barely a warmth, a spark grown cold.
But in that flicker, there's a choice,
A whispered prayer, a quiet voice.
Will you fight, or let it fall?
The final flicker, the final call.
The flame that flickers, it begs for life,
Yet stands alone, surrounded by strife.
It fights the dark, it fights the night,
But can't escape the endless flight.
And so it fades, the light is gone,
The final flicker, the dying song.
A world once bright, now swallowed whole,
A flicker lost, a silent soul.
The darkness claims, the night is king,
A final flicker, the end it brings.

20. The Last Breath

The final breath, it leaves so slow,
A whisper soft, a gentle blow.
The life once held, now slips away,
The end of all, the final day.
The air grows thick, the pulse grows weak,
A shallow sigh, a silence deep.
The breath once full, now lost, now gone,
A fleeting echo, a quiet song.
The last breath comes, no struggle, no fight,
It simply fades into the night.
No more words, no more tears,
Just the calm that follows fears.
But in that breath, there's peace, there's grace,
A stillness found, a final place.
No more pain, no more strife,
Just the quiet end of life.
And so we breathe, we let it go,
The final breath, the softest flow.
The world is still, the soul is free,
The last breath calls, eternally.
The air is still, the pulse has ceased,
A final breath, a soul at peace.

21. The Final Question

Beneath the weight of broken skies,
Where *Shadows Linger*, silence cries.
The *Flicker of the Forgotten*, it fades,
Lost in *The Silent Scream* it made.
Echoes of the Hollow ring,
Where *The End is Only a Beginning*.
Whispers of the Dying, soft and low,
Tell tales of where we dare not go.
From *The Heart That Never Stops* to *The Path of Empty
Light*,
We wander through the *Shadows of the Night*.
The Weight of It All pulls us down,
A crown of *Thorns* that won't let us drown.
The Dust of Time settles thick,
As we search for answers, *quick, quick, quick*.
The Long Road, *The Final Flicker*, we follow,
Into *The Last Breath*, where hearts are hollow.
We move, we dream, we fight, we fall,
But does it matter? Does it all?
We dance through time, chasing the sun,
But in the end, are we ever done?
In the quiet, the final stillness comes—
A whisper lost, a song unsung.
We stand before it, the truth untold,

The questions, the answers, they unfold.
What is life, if not to break?
What is love, if not a fake?
And in the end, when we're left alone,
Is peace just a lie we've always known?
Epitaphs of a Dying Sun—
Is it an end, or just the run?
A final echo, a fleeting thought,
Or the truth we've always sought?